SHADOWS OF WAR ⁓ A GERMAN SOLDIER'S LOST PHOTOGRAPHS OF WORLD WAR II ⁓

[*Willi Rose* EDITED AND WITH AN INTRODUCTION BY *Thomas Eller* ESSAY BY *Petra Bopp*]

HARRY N. ABRAMS, INC., PUBLISHERS

PAGE 3: A British infantry tank captured by German soldiers

PROJECT MANAGER: Christopher Sweet
EDITOR: Sigi Nacson
DESIGNER: Brankica Kovrlija
IMAGE PROCESSING: Bill Jourdan, Ada-Boy Productions
PRODUCTION MANAGER: Justine Keefe

LIBRARY OF CONGRESS CATALOGING-IN-PUBLICATION DATA

Rose, Willi.
  Shadows of war : a German soldier's lost photographs of World War II / Willi Rose ;
edited and with an introduction by Thomas Eller ; essay by Petra Bopp.
      p. cm.
  Includes bibliographical references and index.
  ISBN 0-8109-5590-3 (hardcover)
  1. World War, 1939-1945—Campaigns—Eastern Front—Pictorial works. 2.
Soldiers—Germany—Pictorial works. I. Eller, Thomas, 1964- II. Bopp, Petra. III.
Title.

  D764.R654 2004
  940.54'21'0222—dc22

                        2004015403

Published in 2004 by Harry N. Abrams, Incorporated, New York.

PRINTED AND BOUND IN SINGAPORE

10 9 8 7 6 5 4 3 2 1

HARRY N. ABRAMS, INC.
100 Fifth Avenue
New York, N.Y. 10011
www.abramsbooks.com

Abrams is a subsidiary of
LA MARTINIÈRE

ACKNOWLEDGEMENTS

Just a few years ago it would have been impossible to publish this collection of images. While the photographs are the same, our perspective on them has changed. Many circumstances helped pave the way. W. G. Sebald's book *On the Natural History of Destruction* introduced an array of issues that challenge the way we think about the historical ascription of victim and perpetrator roles. And as I remain very suspicious of the attempts at easy vindication by the likes of Jörg Friedrich—his book *Der Brand* misses the diligence required for such delicate subject matter—there are more sides to history. We are more willing to look deeper into the gray areas of reality where the individual and the historical coincide and nobody can get away innocent.

Without this cultural shift, I think this collection would not have gained its relevance. Coinciding also with a wider discussion on soldiers' photography fuelled by very current events, this book continues in a field that was mapped out by Susan Sontag thirty years ago in her book *On Photography*.

This book also owes its existence to a chain of lucky coincidences. Had not my great-aunt Emilie Rose and my grandmother Alice Rose decided to hand the photographs over to me, and had I not met my friend and publisher Christopher Sweet, the project would never have existed. Without the detective work of my father, Heinz Eller, the interviews with the veterans from the Ninety-Seventh Infantry Division in Munich would have been hard to organize from New York. I owe a lot of insight into soldiers' photography to Petra Bopp. Her expertise provides the frame in which this book can exist. Michael Toennissen, a student of history, helped compile and organize the timeline and captions for the images.

Finally it is my great-uncle Willi Rose that I have to be grateful to for taking and preserving the photographs. His vision, not his morality, is the foundation for this book.

—THE

INTRODUCTION [*Thomas Eller*]

CENTRAL PARK WEST, ROOFTOP, NEW YORK, SUMMER OF 1995. "Thomas, for a German, you're a really nice guy!"—I let a couple of seconds pass. This had come so unexpectedly—my mind was racing to find an answer. "Oh, thank you," I finally replied, as if flattered, and I managed to maneuver around this odd remark.

I had arrived in New York a couple of weeks before. My thick accent, still noticeable today, must have made me reminiscent of the villains in many Hollywood movies. It is hard to get away from cultural stereotypes. It's visceral—before the recognition of another individual can ever set in, we have already arrived at a judgment. My presence on that rooftop, with fantastic views of the city on a gorgeous summer evening, must have first triggered and then shattered somebody's reference system, hence the expression of surprise. "... for a German ...!" Probably this friend of a friend didn't even realize the conundrum he threw me into. How does a German relate to his own German-ness?

This was only the first in a longer line of such events. And though they became less pronounced and poignant in time, less frequent too, they never ceased. Growing up in Germany we used to dodge this question. There was almost a feeling of superiority in avoiding it. My generation really believed in riding the cusp of progress by claiming to be instead citizens of the world. No, we were not Germans! Denying one's own nationality is an attitude so German it might actually serve as a definition of contemporary German-ness. On the other end of the spectrum, a sentence like "I'm proud to be German" would put one deep into fascist territory. In the U.S. anyone stating the same about being American would be absolutely acceptable.

MY PARENTS' LIVING ROOM, MÜRSBACH, GERMANY, WINTER OF 2000. "I thought, maybe, you would like to take a look at these," said my grandmother in her indirect and always terribly understated way, as she slowly climbed the stairs on her eighty-year-old feet, her hands clutching a dilapidated shoe box. In her voice was an all-too-familiar promise reminiscent of the times in my childhood when she would show me the sweetest berries in the garden for the tenth time. What was she bringing?

My grandmother put the cardboard box into my hands. Opening it, I found a cache of about five hundred photographs taken by one of her older brothers, Willi, during his time as a motorcycle messenger on the German front in the Soviet Union during World War II. This was the information that came with the box and also that his widow didn't want them anymore. Eight years after his death, she could no longer bear the presence of the photographs in her house, yet complied with his wish not to throw them away.

I can't remember my great uncle Willi ever holding a camera. In fact I didn't know him very well. He was present at the usual family gatherings: birthdays, Christmas, Easter. He was very quiet, almost shy, but seemed to have a lot of sympathy for everyone around the table. There was always a smile on his face. My mother, I know, was very close to him. But he never spoke up or shared many of his thoughts. He sat and watched. With the warmth that he radiated, he appeared to be the quintessential good uncle.

Now there were the photographs, and they stunned me. All of them basically contact prints from 6 x 9-cm negatives, they were of excellent quality. The way they were shot, the perspectives, the moments were so surprising, the compositions beyond the capabilities of the average amateur photographer. I was mystified.

And I didn't understand them—at all. Lots of rivers with naked soldiers loafing around, lots of landscapes, some civilians, campsites, a lot of soldiers marching . . . three swastikas only and just one dead body. A stark distortion of World War II, or so it seemed. But then again, how does one take a picture of war? Can there be a general picture of war? Can there at least be *pictures* of war? There are of course all the official ones that we grew up with; the ones that we, as a society, gave ourselves after the war; the ones that create order and divide the world into good and bad. Created after the fact and distant, they could judge. But how do you take a picture from within?—those were some of my immediate questions.

The images stunned me, all five hundred of them. I don't remember if they were in any particular order when I first got them. I was so electrified I poured them all out onto the table to find the "best" images from a purely artistic point of view. I found a Manet, a Rodchenko, a Sergei Eisenstein, but I couldn't tell if any particular image was shot in France, Slovakia, the Ukraine, Poland, or Russia. Of course, I regretted this mistake dearly when I started going deeper into trying to understand the images.

Fortunately, almost all the photographs bear markings, handwritten numbering systems, on their backs. Very few of them have notes referring to their subjects. In order to attain a more or less impartial, unedited order I turned the images face down and sorted them according to the markings that I believed to be notes by the photo lab, where Willi had them printed. I could identify about nine distinct groups of photos that differed in the quality of paper used, the cut of the borders, and the markings on the backs. The most extensive series accounts for 136 images of the entire collection and seems in itself to be almost complete. Numbered from 1 through 137, only four numbers are missing, and three numbers had been erroneously assigned twice. Turning the images face up did indeed make sense. There are the batches of images that are clearly from France. Much to my later surprise, the two images of camels that I assumed were taken in the south of France, were in fact taken on the Kuban lowlands of southern Russia. I used the road signs in some of the photos to approximate where and also when the photos must have been taken, which became possible after my father started researching the history of Willi

Rose's division. That was an interesting collaboration: My father was looking at documents—I was looking at images. It almost seems that, besides our personal division of labor, this also represents a generational shift.

After a while I was able to read photos that hadn't made sense before. A group of four images showing a flooded village and the damage afterward more or less from the same vantage point were curious—why would my great uncle take photos of the flood and then return the next day or even later to take a photo again? What was the significance? There is no proof of course, but a likely assumption would suggest this to be the bombing of the Manytch dam by the retreating Soviet Army, trying to drown German soldiers. Not always providing hard evidence, the images nonetheless started speaking about certain events: The tank battle of Magerov, the battles for Artemovsk and Alexandrovka. Other images were much clearer. I researched the memorials for the fallen soldiers of World War I near Verdun. It was easy to unearth the story of the battleship *L'Adroit* and the battle for Dunkirk. Also the Hotchkiss tank, built for the French army by a former American company, gave away its story quite readily. A photo of Soviet landmines was deciphered with the help of Frank Masche, who runs a Web site against the use of landmines. As if in a giant game of memory, I was flipping back and forth through the images linking different batches of images to the same events, finding duplicates for weeks. The more I knew about the images, the deeper I was drawn into the history of World War II, and the more the images puzzled me. Three swastikas and one dead body—against an estimated twenty-one million dead Russians. From the perspective of this collection of images, war seemed like a prolonged summer camp. Or did it? The omissions were all too noticeable. Because of the aesthetic qualities, or, as a friend put it, "I'm always thinking I'm looking at art," a strange bewilderment was seeping in. The photos by Willi Rose are visually pleasing. Is it what's not seen that makes for the horrors of war (invisible *Désastres de la Guerre*)? Or is it his eye? The cold, uncanny eye of the photographer that distances the world. Some of Willi's photos even breathe the same air as Moholy-Nagy's elegantly detached images.

Where is the photographer? On many levels this has become the recurring question for me in the face of Willi Rose's photographs. At first it was really only about comprehension: Where did he take the photos? Which places did he see? The personal: What was Willi Rose doing? A couple of photos show him and the other important device besides the camera, the motorcycle. It seems he depended on both to get through the war. Other photos show him shaving, eating, hiding out with a friend. Or the technical: Where was the camera positioned? A lot of the photos were shot from unusual perspectives, from down below or high up. To see the camera move is one the most exciting aspects of this collection. At times, the camera revolves around its subject, zooming in on the most significant shot. On other occasions there are sequences that record entire events; for example, the capturing and disarming of Soviet soldiers. The sense of urgency that is created by those formal decisions is what carries the idea of war photography. In the absence of gruesome detail, it's the acuity of those visual decisions that also means combat.

Where is the photographer? Through all the above questions, do I get a clearer picture of my great-uncle? Is the collection of photographs an answer to what else he must have seen?

BNAI ZION FOUNDATION, EAST THIRTY-NINTH STREET, NEW YORK, OCTOBER 2003. An invitation card had arrived out of nowhere: "Reconnaissance Photographs of World War II." The exhibition and opening ceremony took place in a 1960s conference room, renovated in the eighties with wall-to-wall carpeting and huge air-conditioner vents. There was a buffet in the center of the space and a stage at the rear end of the room underneath the banner of the foundation. In a corner, the American and Israeli flags. Everybody in the room, with a few exceptions, was in their mid-eighties. Jewish-American veterans of World War II. Some of them in uniform, even with guns on their belts. "There are still people who claim the Holocaust never happened. We were there, we saw it. We are living proof it existed." After thirty minutes the speeches were over and the exhibition opened. I was so apprehensive I could not talk to anyone there. While I was looking at the photos, people started mingling. Someone played a medley on the piano, old melodies of the thirties and forties that I didn't really pay too much attention to. When he began playing "Lili Marleen," tears shot up to my eyes and I left.

Back to the photographs: Turning them face down again. Are there any more clues behind the images? What I couldn't explain for the longest time was that some series carried more than one indexing system. Maybe those are not marks from the photo lab at all. The different indices suggest that the images had been rearranged up to three, four times. What I didn't know in the beginning was that soldiers at the front lines taking photos held little fairs, trading them amongst themselves. Obviously some of the groups of Willi Rose's photos had been in more than one such event. The different numbers very rarely showed longer sequences anymore. Some were just reiterated, as if to identify the author/owner of the photographs. It is highly probable that not all the photos in Willi Rose's collection were also taken by him. Are those with multiple indices his, because he presented them more than once? Is the large and most comprehensive series his? It contains even redundant photos one wouldn't acquire if one could choose only the best photos. Hard to tell. Did he take the images at all? His camera still exists. It is an American camera: Kodak Jr. Six-20 Series III, f-6.3 105 mm, which was manufactured between 1938 and 1939, supporting the theory that he is, in fact, the *author* of the photos in his collection.

KAMERADSCHAFTSTREFFEN DER SPIELHAHNJÄGER, GASTHOF RAETHENHAUS, MUNICH, JANUARY 2004. Once every month veterans from the Ninety-seventh Infantry Division meet at this restaurant to maintain the bond forged among them during the war. "Willi Rose? Two hundred and fourth regiment?" One of the veterans could remember my great-uncle. My father had researched the address of the veterans' club and we were invited to meet them. Another room filled with men in their mid-eighties. No uniforms this time. I passed around photos, asking them to help me read the images. They were very good at identifying their generals and sergeants; as for locations, with one exception, I didn't learn more. They gave us three books about the division, which provided many clues and did help connect images to certain events. While I was sitting there talking to quite a few of them, my mind was on the photos of young soldiers. Nothing seemed militaristic about them anymore, yet they were the ones who had fought in the Caucasus, Crimea, and the Carpathian Mountains. When we left, their chairman bid us farewell: "And please! Don't call us murderers again! We weren't!"

With authorship called into question on all levels, how does one explain how things could have happened the way they did? As a German, does one have to have committed a crime of war to be guilty, or is being German enough? In the case of the person Willi Rose, my great-uncle, when I saw him emerge from those images, he was vanishing again behind the wall of images. What was his contribution?

I realize my resistance to this uncertainty. I wanted to be able to connect on a personal level to the story of the images. I'm also realizing that the problem of being German has to do with guilt that can be dealt with only by creating exactly this uncertainty: Who was the author? I would like to say: Willi Rose took those photos. Problem is, I can't. From a distance, from the U.S., things appear different. In all likelihood, this book would not exist had I not moved to New York, a place outside the uncertainty that Germany entertains; New York that confronted me with the reality of my history.

⁖ ⁖

Since the viability of photographs as documents is very much in question here (without context, the viewer is free to interpret according to his knowledge or predilection), I am using them as visual material for a recomposition. The Parisian historian Ruggiero Romano suggests that rather than documents, photographs are monuments, because they serve as vessels for our memories. Out of the 500 or so photographs, about 230 were chosen to compose a dense visualization of the war, with the hope that the juxtapositions will lead to a realization of what is not shown. To that end I departed from the idea of a chronological or thematic order. This book will be a monument to German uncertainty.

VIEWING THE PHOTOGRAPHS OF WILLI ROSE [Petra Bopp]

"Some fog spots cannot be resolved by the eye." JEAN PAUL

THE SHADOW OF THE PHOTOGRAPHER falling onto a village street. The eye of the camera aiming at two soldiers in lockstep, arms linked with one another, and flashing smiles toward the lens. Behind them two small girls dressed in white walking hand in hand shielding their eyes from the sun and from the photographer's gaze. A little boy disappearing within the dark shadow cast by the soldiers' bodies; in the background are a couple of houses and two women with children.

How can we approach this photo today, made by a German soldier during World War II? How to look at small visual relics—taken from private collections and brought into the realm of a book-reading public? What happens when one readjusts the focus, thus bringing the blurry photos into sharper definition?—when artists, historians, and art historians set out to search for the buried traces of a photo collection and dare to stage a test arrangement? Another fragment in the cosmos of the microhistory of national socialism is ready for documentation. At the same time, the photos speak for themselves as symbolic images.

We know very little about the context of these photos' creation. Merely from the numbering and notations on the backs of the photos one can assume that this photo might have been taken in France, circa 1940. A bundle of five hundred photos sends us into a labyrinth of memories, visual aphorisms, curiosity, amazement, and horror. Since the photographer's oral narration is missing and due to the fact that he did not tell a story of his own about these snapshots in an album from five years of war experiences, sixty years later our gaze can wander freely over them. It can delve into motifs that, although alien to us, do not let us go. It can expose us to aesthetic stimuli that are familiar to us from entirely different and contemporary image patterns. Unassuming photographs are now compiled in a book for a story, to form a sequence, to offer a possible reading. Viewpoints result from the combination of single photos, interrelations open up from situations. But stopping at random while browsing, comparative speculating, and accidental straying are imaginable as well, since the puzzlelike labor of reconstructing the recognizable leads us down the garden path again and again. It leaves us standing in the foggy patches of that which can only be imagined.

Why is Willi Rose lying down in the grass to take a photo of a barbed-wire fence (p. 150)? The motif—by today's perception more linked to seconds-long newscast segments from the conflict zones of this world such as Guantanamo, Israel/Palestine, Cyprus, Iraq—engrained itself deep into the collective cultural memory with the metaphor-laden images of Nazi concentration camps during national socialism. Rose photographs the weathered old fence from an accentuated view from below so that the barbed wire cuts the image in half diagonally in one photo while looming up as a tangled ball in the other, forming an upside-down heart through coincidental tangling. While most comparable images show those segregated behind the fence as well, the motif in these photos seems to have been photographed for its graphic appeal. Yet, in the context of the images of war, it is charged with aggression and trauma. Artistic representations of war, such as Paul Nash's paintings from World War I and Sigalit Landau's video *Barbed Hula* dealing with the Israel/Palestine conflict, support the painful experiences described by photographers with this metaphor of segregation and violence. Viewed against this background, Rose's small photographs lead us deep into a different form of perception, the one of a private view into World War II.

Already in 1933 Joseph Goebbels declared private photography an important means of propaganda and called for an "army of millions of amateur photographers for the unlimited and nationally important area of spiritual and mental labor of reconstruction" (Frerk, p. 417). In doing so, "primarily the German woman" was supposed to be "called upon to secure a new place for photography within family life. Not the man but the woman shall be the creator of the German family image." (Stephainsky, p. 229) This calling was repeated at the beginning of the war, once again with gender-specific role allocation: "Our women should take more photos." (Koristka, p. 334) "Likewise it is an absolute duty of the soldier . . . not to let the camera rest right now. " (Starke, p. 349) Consequently, the photos became—along with the usual field-post mail—a popular means of transfer for the particular experiences on the western, eastern, southern, and home fronts. In 1939 about ten percent of the German population

 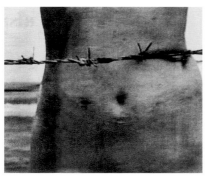

LEFT: Paul Nash, *Wire* (1918/19), oil on canvas, 71.4 x 91.7 cm, Imperial War Museum London. In: *"Kunst und Krieg"* (Art and War), *Kunstforum*, vol. 165, 2003, p. 91. RIGHT: Sigalit Landau, "Barbed Hula, 2000", color still from 2-minute DVD.; in: *Dagens Nyheter*, Stockholm, February 22, 2003.

owned a camera, totaling seven million people. Many participated in "Photography for Everyone" courses in order to learn the "correct" technique and composition. The goal of this "attempt at streamlining the public and private image worlds" according to Party standards (*Gleichschaltung*) was the abolition of differences between amateurs organized in associations and snapshooters, because "photography is the writing by image of the people" and everybody speaks the same language; however, "every race has its own photo language." (Stiewe, pp. 9, 16) This mixing of semipublic and semiprivate image worlds was greatly intensified through the situation at the front. The classification of private—snapshooter/amateur—and public—professional propaganda photography—depends mainly on the conditions of creation as well as on means of distribution and reception. Besides Goebbels calling on the snapshooters, the setting-up of *Propaganda-Kompanien* (propaganda companies or PKs) for the professional coverage of the war in word and image was of decisive importance for media procurement. All photographs, articles, and film underwent double censorship: that of the military and that of the *Reichsministerium für Volksaufklärung und Propaganda* (Reich Ministry for the Enlightenment of the People and Propaganda).

The propaganda photographers were professionals bringing around their own *"Bildzug"* (image wagon), a special vehicle for equipment, film material, and development. The PK photographers received precise instructions as to what was to be photographed and how: advancing troops always from left to right (because Poland and Russia were in the east, which is on the right side of a map) and combat photos from an elevated point of view because the German soldier was more highly developed and therefore dominated the scene. The propaganda companies were integral parts of the individual armies and, as a general rule, were deployed on the front lines. Combat propaganda, troop care, and war coverage were part of their duties. They supported the soldiers who took pictures so that an active exchange of photos took place within the regiments. The soldiers could order prints—made from negatives created on official assignments—from the propaganda companies for their own private use. The subject matter and professional handling of the camera surely had an influence on the representation of the snapshot-taking soldiers. These trading and ordering activities were also common among the soldiers themselves, therefore it is not certain in the case of the preserved sequences that the photos were all taken by the same photographer. Ambitious amateur photographers in turn often gave their prints to the propaganda regiments for further use. These gray areas of proper authorship need to be kept in mind while looking at today's traditional photo collections. While the PK photographers had to follow clear instructions and while their photos would be furnished with texts only after passing censorship and being reproduced in completely different contexts, the snapshooters and amateur photographers could choose their motifs freely and tell their own stories of the war in their war albums.

In many ways the photo collection of Willi Rose is consistent with the popular picture motifs of soldiers' albums: landscapes in France, landmarks in Paris, then the advance into the Soviet Union, the civil population in the occupied countries, prisoners of war, soldiers' everyday life, destruction, burning villages, death. Following this narrative pattern of many albums, Rose's photographs, too, could be arranged to tell a story. But his way of composing the subjects in the picture is striking. Between the group shots and the depictions of landscape, the gaze again and again comes to rest upon mysterious phenomena: in one image a dark object rises with the smoke of the burning houses and hovers apocalyptically above the fire (p. 114). Reason enough for Rose to photograph it in full frame, to record the inferno in an unimposing small square photo. This square symbolizes the horror, and the threat in abstract form detaches itself completely from the recognizable object.

In order to represent the advance of the German infantry, Rose adopts the large-scale diagonal as has been recommended to the PK photographers. Because he served with the bicycle platoon, IR 204 of the Ninety-Seventh Light Infantry Division, or *Spielhahnjägerdivision* (Black Cock Hunter Division), in 1941, he first went to Slovakia, then to the Ukraine. Three photos (pp. 66–67) show how soldiers advanced far into the country with armaments and bicycles, across grasslands and sandy terrain. Rose shoots the groups from behind, leading the gaze of the beholder past the repoussoir figures and into the space of the landscape conquered by the soldiers. Completely in accordance with the PK instructions, a group of soldiers behind a covered wagon moves on foot from the picture's left to the right (p. 62). The

Alexander Rodchenko, *Dive into Water*, 1934; in: Alexander Lavrentiev, *Alexander Rodchenko, Photography 1924–1954*, Cologne, 1995, no. 200.

horsemen in two photos (pp. 64–65) move in the opposite direction, from the foreground's right side to the left side of the background. Horse and horseman are silhouetted sharply and darkly against the bright sky. This backlit effect was a popular art technique employed by professional as well as amateur photographers. Thus the PK photographer Walter Henisch raves about his own photographs of the Soviet Union and the Balkans: "Just look at the sky—see how the clouds come forward? This conveys an unforgettable impression of the vastness of the Russian landscape. I used a yellow filter—yes, yes on purpose. . . . Backlighting was always my specialty" (Henisch, p. 83). Rose composes two photographs of a tank (pp. 73, 75) as the apotheosis of the advance. Driving head-on toward the photographer and in large-scale landscape format, engulfed in the street's dust and with four soldiers in pyramidal formation, the photograph conveys combat effectiveness, strength, and determination. The image of the tank from behind, nearly disappearing completely in the dust, still enhances the impression of the speed of the advance.

The many photographs of river crossings illuminate the theme of penetrating into a foreign country. Soldiers repeatedly build artificial crossings and bridges across the wide rivers Dniepr, Don, and Manytch in the Ukraine. Rubber rafts are deployed to create temporary bridges for bicycles, horse-drawn wagons, and men. A series of six snapshots (pp. 98–101), of the pushing, hauling, splashing, naked soldiers shows that in the summer's heat there were also funny scenes to shoot.

Only a few photographs reproduce the wide landscapes of the Soviet Union. The signposts of the *Wehrmacht* (armed forces), keeping things grounded optically—and in reality, too—seem to have been far more important to the photographer than landscapes: the Black Cock Hunter Division emblem, the feather twisted to the left, comes to the fore as a motif four times (pp. 144–145, 155). They are the national emblem and markings of the conquerors in the occupied country. A deadly practice is concealed in the photographs of mines (p. 149) and of the sign *'Minen-Frei'* (free of mines, p. 148): in order to detonate the Soviet antitank and antipersonnel mines, people were chased across the mined terrain as *'Minensuchgerät 42'* (mine detectors 42). "Because one has to anticipate mines, one has to arrange for the allocation of mine detectors 42 (Jews or captured gang members with harrows and cylinders) in adequate quantities. The units have to equip themselves with ropes in order to furnish the Jews or gang members with long ropes connected to

nooses around their necks" (Operational Order 532 of the Commander of the Army Territory Behind the Lines, 9/9/1942).

The most popular themes of every album are the representations of one's own comrades and superiors. Rose depicts the war's beginnings in France with chipper group shots (p. 29), with soldiers dining at set tables (p. 40), and lining up with their legs apart in front of a café (p. 38). Rowing is represented as a leisure-time activity in an idyllic river landscape (p. 29) and a group of card-players is sitting contentedly at a table (p. 52). These images tie in with the standardized motifs of private photography associated with family albums, class shots, photos of family festivities, and leisure-time activities such as sports and traveling.

On the eastern front the customs get tougher, the everyday life of soldiers more arduous. Ordinary activities such as eating and shaving are represented in unusual situations (pp. 53, 165). Photos of the business of war prevail: briefings (pp. 161–162), communications troops (pp. 87–89), evacuation of the wounded (pp. 152–153), and funerals (pp. 42, 154).

An important motif of all photographs made on the eastern front are the encounters with the civil population and the capture of soldiers of the Red Army. While Rose photographed the Algerian prisoners of the French colonial troops within the group of German soldiers, he used the image patterns of the PK photographers, as they could often be seen in the German press whenever he photographed the Soviet prisoners of war. In order to emphasize the high number of

LEFT: Francisco José de Goya y Lucientes, *The Shooting of the Insurgents in Madrid on May 3, 1808* (1814), oil on canvas, 266 x 345 cm, Prado, Madrid. RIGHT: Edouard Manet, *The Shooting of the Emperor Maximilian* (1868/69), oil on canvas, 252 x 302 cm, Städtische Kunsthalle Mannheim.

captives, the soldiers of the Red Army are shown either marching as a guarded column or as a huge amorphous mass in an open field (pp. 138, 143). Snapshots show the surrendering soldiers with hands held up high and a white flag on one of their rifles being frisked (pp. 134, 139). In this way, Rose succeeds in taking a photograph (p. 137) that is reminiscent of Robert Capa's *The Death of a Loyalist Militiaman, Cerro Muriano, 1936.* The representation of the gesture with arms held high as a sign of submission, terror, and death gains its explosive effect through the unseen perpetrator and his gun, imagined to be outside of the picture, to the right. In Rose's depiction, the point of view of the photographer is also that of the aggressor with pistol or rifle forcing surrender on the Soviet soldiers. The often violent snapshot can come before the shot from a pistol: "These home movies and stills were usually of relatively poor quality; they were often shot by murderers who minutes later killed the people they had just photographed." (Milton, p. 48) In the famous history painting *May 3, 1808*, which shows the shooting of Spanish insurgents by Napoleonic troops, Goya repre-

sents the Spanish patriot with exactly this gesture of arms held up high on the left side of the picture, while the shooting soldiers are shown on the right. Manet repeats this arrangement in his painting *The Shooting of the Emperor Maximilian* from 1868/69. Paul Klee reduces this scene to two persons—perpetrator and victim, the shooter and the person shot—in the drawing *Violence* from 1933.

Simultaneously with Rose, the PK-image reporter Gerhard Gronefeld photographed this subject during the execution of hostages at the cemetery wall in Pančevo, Serbia, on April 22, 1941. The photograph shows an officer of the armed forces regiment "Grossdeutschland" (Greater Germany), aiming his pistol at a dying victim. This photograph became the icon of the first *Wehrmachtsausstellung* (an exhibition about the German armed forces' involvement in crimes of war during World War II) after being rendered as a drawing on the cover of the March 10th edition of *Der Spiegel* magazine in 1997. As an explicit portrayal of a perpetrator, this image can be seen as a complementary element to Rose's photograph. The aforementioned examples embody an aggregation of motifs that could be described as pathos formula in the context of Aby Warburg's iconological theory. The concentration of visual occurrences of this gesture between 1933 and 1943—in Klee's drawing, Capa's and Gronefeld's professional photography, as well as Rose's snapshot—represent a contemporary historical manifestation going back to predecessors such as Goya and Manet. Thus a supratemporal dimension of the motif reveals itself.

There are portrait shots of captives that have been published often in the German press since World War I. The photograph of the foreign soldier circulated as a caricature on postcards and in large illustrated books (Reetz, 1934). The depictions of the "savage on the European theater of war" (*Illustrierte Zeitung*,

12/24/1914) were further developed over time (Bauer, 1933) and contrasted with the hard, determined profile photo of the German soldier of the *Wehrmacht* (Ehlert 1933).

During the twenties and thirties and against the backdrop of early colonial photography, extensive portfolios had been developed in order to showcase Germans and their environments. While August Sander was committed to a collection of portraits organized by class with an emphasis on an objective form of photography, Erna Lendvai-Dircksen executed her collections of the "German and Germanic Face of the People" between 1930 and 1944 with racist objectives. Different attitudes toward the portrayed reveal themselves in her work through the use of top or bottom views or via the direct head-on shot. Willi Rose

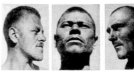

LEFT: *Der Spiegel*, cover, March 10, 1997. Pencil drawing of a Gerhard Groenfeld photograph, Pančevo, April 1941. MIDDLE: Max Ehlert, "Zwei Männer für ein Ziel" (Two Men for One Goal), *Berliner Illustrierte Zeitung*, no. 36, September 10, 1933; in: Ed. Bodo von Dewitz, *Kiosk. Eine Geschichte der Fotoreportage 1839–1973* (*Kiosk*. A History of Photo Reportage 1839–1973), Göttingen, 2001, p. 163. RIGHT: Friedrich Franz Bauer, *"Die Wahrheit über Dachau"* (The Truth about Dachau), detail, *Münchner Illustrierte Presse*, no. 28, July 16, 1933; in: Ed. Bodo von Dewitz, Kiosk. *Eine Geschichte der Fotoreportage 1839–1973* (*Kiosk*. A History of Photo Reportage 1839–1973), Göttingen, 2001, p. 171.

varies the possibilities. In the group portraits (pp. 140–141) he faces the prisoners at eye level, and in the single portrait (p. 142) he accentuates the head with the chiaroscuro created by photographing the subject from below against the sky. The portrait of the commander of the Second Infantry Regiment 207, Captain Karl Langesee (p. 147), is composed in a similar way. It was also taken from below so that the German officer and the Soviet prisoner of war were surprisingly portrayed in the same way.

Rose shows the destructive effects of the war on the German *Wehrmacht* with photos of burning houses, landscapes going up in smoke, and burned vehicles. There are only two photos of dead horses and one of a dead Soviet soldier (pp. 156–157). This indicates that Rose abided closely by the rules and prohibitions set for photographers by the supreme command of the *Wehrmacht* and of the *Waffen-SS* (Weapons-SS): "It is prohibited to take photos of executions in and outside of the territory of the (Third) *Reich*" (Ordinance Paper of the Weapons-SS, 6/15/1941). "It is prohibited for all members of the *Wehrmacht* to take photos of executions, shooting as well as hanging, as well as to take photos of the bodies of dead Russian soldiers. It is further prohibited to send such prints already in existence to the homeland because it is highly undesirable that photos of such unaesthetic subject matter be distributed among the civil population" (Commander of the *Wehrmacht*, East Territory/White Ruthenia, Special Order No. 55, 12/13/1941). Photos of hanged and shot people, of traces of the Holocaust, and of the war of extermination led by the German *Wehrmacht* in the east are to be found in many war albums, archives, and PK

LEFT: August Sander, "Young Farmers, c. 1920"; in: Ed. Gunther Sander, *August Sander. Menschen des 20. Jahrhunderts. Portraitfotografien 1892–1952* (August Sander. People of the Twentieth Century. Portrait Photography 1892–1952), Munich, 1980, no. 16. RIGHT: Ordinance Paper of the Weapons-SS, June 15, 1941, detail; in: Peter Jahn, Ulrike Schmiegelt, *Foto-Feldpost. Geknipste Kriegserlebnisse 1939–1945* (Photo Army Mail. Snapshots of War Experiences 1939–1945), Berlin: Elefanten Presse, 2000, p. 75.

photos. Rose does not show this; instead he uses the images of the toppled German tank jammed in the ditch (pp. 130–131), of the destroyed trucks, trains, planes (pp. 56, 69, 127, 133) to reveal the horrors of war. Two shots of bicycles lying in the grass appear to be transposed into the metaphorical (pp. 43, 151). The empty area of grass in the middle is zoomed in on, with blurred edges, and can be seen as a projection screen for absence, silence, death.

The plainest references to the destruction caused by the German *Wehrmacht* can be found in the shots of burning farmhouses (pp. 117–119). Since 1941, villages had been evacuated and burned for reasons of the so-called struggle against gangs: "The ordered torching of localities on the front line and in the forefront has been initiated and will be advanced by all means. It is at once prohibited for the male civil population to leave the localities in any way. . . . Every male civilian outside of the confines of the village is to be shot." (War Diary of the Seventy-fifth Infantry Division Ic, 12/23/1941 and January 1942). These measures of declaring "dead zones" were propelled further from 1943 on during the retreat. The policy of the "scorched earth" was utilized in order to "deprive the enemy of access to the entire civilian population for the purposes of military service and labor and to preserve resources for the employment of labor in the service of the *Reich*" (Tank Army High Command 3 on the Civilian Population in the Evacuation Case of Vitebsk, 2/13/1944). An encrypted message from the Combat Group Knecht during the "Partisan Operation Winter Magic" in February 1943 gives clear instructions on the procedures, as can be deduced from Rose's photographs: "Whenever possible, necessary executions should be left to the SD (*Sicherheitsdienst*, or Security Services) so that executions can be conducted in a way that leaves no traces. In the case that executions need to be carried out by ordinary troops due to the SD not being close by, the execution has to take place inside houses. The dead bodies are to be covered with straw or hay and shall be burned in the houses" (Berta 2/18/1943). Two night photos (pp. 116–117) point at Rose's heightened interest in this motif. The PK photographer Walter Henisch comments on his own photographs of the same procedure in a cynical fashion: ". . . these Panje huts set on fire by shots. Aside from everything else—isn't it a magnificent motif? The silhouette of the German soldier in front of the red-hot burning truss!" (Henisch, p. 82 et seq.)

The photographs of the deserted, scenic landscapes of the "desert zones" with the smoke-covered horizon line (pp. 108, 112) remind today's viewer of historical photographs of the Crimean War (Roger Fenton, *The Valley of the Shadow of Death*, 1855) as well as of World War I, and of television images and photos from the Iraq and Afghanistan wars of recent years.

"Soldier's photography is the mosaic work of documenting a military campaign, which allows for the direct connection with the homeland and, later, the preservation of the valuable memories. . . . Naturally one abstains from prohibited photos, such as details of weapons and fortifications, because these could find their way into the wrong hands. These photos are

LEFT: Roger Fenton, *The Valley of the Shadow of Death*, Crimea, 1855. RIGHT: *War Alert*, Video Still of Live Images of War; in: *"Kunst und Krieg"* (Art and War), *Kunstforum*, vol. 165, 2003, p. 110.

taken and utilized from a completely different point of view. The soldier rather limits himself to reporting on his own person; the homeland will do its own with images of events.... The camera shall be everywhere.... Outside it embodies image reporting, connection with the homeland, mental occupation after physical work—within the homeland it means the continuation of the initiated project of amateur photography, chronicler of the family, connection to the field, and a pleasure-giving eye-animating occupation" (Hummel, pp. 121–122). Rose makes this "eye-animating occupation" a topic in various photographs in which he focuses in on the act of looking itself (pp. 78–79). With field glasses, refracting telescope, and through the viewfinder of a rifle, the transition to actual shooting reveals itself in a short sequence (pp. 76, 80–81). The "view of the belief in absolute power which is deduced from the view through the visor of a weapon" (Hüppauf, p. 516) is transferable to the camera. It keeps the soldier taking photos at a distance from the

subject and makes it possible "to preserve a space for one's self undamaged by the documented horror. It creates the necessity for the depersonalization of the view. Torture that can only be experienced physically is pushed over to the other side of this world divided in two" (Hüppauf, p. 514). Historical events, personal experiences, and cultural knowledge can be decoded in Willi Rose's photos—compiled for today's viewer following the principle of iteration. Aberrantly, through their blurs and irregularities, there emerges a web of aesthetic relationships. Despite the specific contexts of the photographers' creation and perception, this web refers us again and again to the gaps in the mnemonic images and their symbolic value.

Rose's curious view of unusual topics and his joy in experimenting with surprising perspectives (pp. 83, 172) present him as an observant and skillful amateur photographer of this time. Rose often employed the language form of the New View in the Style of New Objectivity developed during the twenties, with its

Alexander Rodchenko, *Electrician on a Pole*, 1929; in: Alexander Lavrentiev,
Alexander Rodchenko, Photography 1924–1954, Cologne, 1995, no. 251.

photographic vocabulary of spatial structures organized by a central perspective, dynamic angular views, extreme diagonals, top and bottom views, effects of light and shadow, and optical structurings (p. 174). Although he stays within the limits of many war albums with his choice of motifs, Rose achieves an impressive consistency in finding his pictures. With a keen eye on the right moment, Rose shoots a scene with two military police and a woman in front of a house (p. 82) in such a way that the shadow of one of the soldiers falls onto the house entrance: the violence and the danger emanating from these men encroaches on the entire scene, transcends the moment, and becomes tangible.

These are the shadows of war becoming visible through all of the smoke screens and blurs. They occupy and disturb our imagination beyond that which is shown.

WILLI ROSE ❖ b. APRIL 30, 1917 — d. MARCH 7, 1992 ❖

TIMELINE

INFORMATION FROM THE DEUTSCHE DIENSTSTELLE (WASt) for the notification of next-of-kin of members of the former German *Wehrmacht*, Berlin

Date of conscription unknown

Identity tag 171 Rdf.Ers.Schwr. 73 in Bamberg

February 1940 In Bicycle Reserve Squadron 73 Bamberg

February 18, 1940 Bicycle Squadron 7 (according to dispatches of November 10, 1940 and November 23, 1940)

December 13, 1940 Infantry Regiment 204/Bicycle Platoon, Weilheim/Oberbayern

August 8, 1944 2nd Company, Field Reserve Battalion 81, Dolhesti (East Carpathians)

November 2, 1944 Baton Regiment, Hunter Regiment 204, northwest of Nizne

November 15, 1944 Cabiny/Slovakia

Service rank Private First Class according to dispatch of April 18, 1943. No date of promotion.

War captivity According to his own statements October 10, 1944–September 10, 1946 (nation of custody not noted).

INQUIRIES

Intelligence Division 7 was deployed on August 2, 1939, in Bamberg for the 7th Infantry Division from the 2nd/Cavalry Regiment 17. On July 29, 1940, the battalion was renamed Bicycle Battalion 7.

Infantry Regiment 204 was deployed on October 15, 1940, from parts of the IR 19 and 61 in Weilheim and subordinated to the Ninety-seventh Light Infantry Division ("Black Cock Hunter Division"; this standard— feather twisted to the left— appears in many photos).

After Willi Rose was ordered to join the 204th Infantry Regiment on December 13, 1940, it would appear that he had been with the 7th Infantry Division before, which, together with the IR 19 or the IR 61, was involved in the campaign against France, even if no dispatch to this end is available.

CHRONICLE OF 1940

May 10 Push to the Meuse Schelde Channel.

May 30 Attack on Lille.

May 31 Relocation to Burgundy.

June 23 Précy.

July 1 Lille-Roubaix.

December 13 Willi Rose is ordered to join Infantry Regiment 204/Bicycle Platoon in Weilheim.

Chronicle of the 204th Infantry Regiment of the 97th Light Infantry Division (aka "Black Cock Hunter Division") during the campaign against Russia 1941–1945, compiled by Michael Toennissen.

1941

June 22 Zamch Tarnogrod area.

June 24 First combat mission near Radruz.

June 27 Combat near Kumin.

June 29 Rest period near Kulików.

July 2 Rest period in Dumajów.

July 14 Breaking through the "Stalin Line" near Tarlóvka.

July 17 Taking of the city of Latjezów.

July 23–26 Taking of the city of Pesochnya.

July 26 Combat near Jarlewzy, Shabel'naya, Vaselevka, and Porchonowka

July 27 Taking of Staryy Dashev; rest period from July 28 until July 31.

July 31 Participation in the battle of encirclement of Uman.

August 7 Podvysokoye.

August 15 Combat near Sanamka.

August 20 Arriving at the Dniepr river near Kremenchuk.

August 31 Construction of a bridge-head in Deriyivka.

September 12 Advance to Poltova via Alexandrovka and Mikhaylovka.

October 20 Combat near Druzhkovka.

End of October Taking of Ivanovskoye in the Donez basin.

November 1 Artemovsk taken; rest period followed.

November 16 Further advance into the east.

December 5 Participation in "Operation Seydlitz;" Deployment of a new main combat line for the subsequent defensive combats. The regiment itself stood near Troitskoye.

1942

January 16 Relocation of the regiment to Artemovsk for rest and recovery.

January 18 Departure from Artemovsk.

During the Soviet counterattack Rose subordinated to the 295th Infantry Division.

February 13 Return of the regiment to the 97th Light Infantry Division.

Combat action in the area of Elyzavetivka, Yavlenskaya, Novo Yakovlevka.

April 1942 Stationed near Sergeyevka for rest and recovery.

May 17 Combat action near Brazhovka.

June 22 Construction of a bridgehead near the Don near Izyum.

July 6 Renaming of the regiment to "Hunter Regiment 204."

July 8 Attack on Mayaky during the course of "Case Blue," the German summer offensive of 1942.

July 21 Battles near Shakhtne, Siambek, and Krasnoznamenka.

July 23 Combat action near Stenka.

July 27 Arrival at the Don.

July 28 Crossing the Don near Bagayevka.

July 29 Crossing the Manytch.

August 13 Taking of Maykop.

August 15 Battles near Chirvanskaya in the Caucasus Mountains.

End of October End of the advance of the regiment at the river Pshish; the Soviet counterattack begun.

December 25–26 Relocation of the regiments to Krasnodar; from then on retreat via Severskaya, Iskaya, Cholmskaya, and Achtyskaya toward Krymskaya.

1943

May 3–4 Retreat toward the "Gothic Line" to the west of Krymskaya. Afterward battles for Moldovanskoye.

September Order to abandon the Kuban bridgehead issued.

October 8 Crossing over to the Crimea.

End of October Retreat via Bolskaya-Lepaticha toward Rubanovka.

1944

Beginning of February Evacuation of the bridgehead near Nikopol.

February 19 Combat action near Voroshilovka.

February 22 Retreat covering 300 km to the Dniestr.

July 6 Regiment becomes part of the army reserve.

July 27 Regiment arrives at Kielce near Bordo.

Beginning of September Relocation to Košice.

November 24 Arrival at "Position Gisela" east of Košice.

1945

January 15 Relocation to Upper Silesia in the area of Katowice for the defense of Eastern Prussia.

January 28 Regiment encircled, but breaks out and fights its way to Ratibor.

January 29 Retreat to "Position Oppa."

End of April–May 8 "Hunter Regiment 204" pushed back via Bielitz, Teschen, Friedeck, and Neutitschen into the area of Prosnitz. It has to capitulate to the Soviet troops near Prague and is captured.

WESTERN FRONT

Willi Rose in a white recruit's uniform during basic training

LEFT: The Loire River near the city of Givors (France)

TOP, LEFT: A French Hotchkiss tank captured by German soldiers TOP AND BOTTOM, RIGHT: A British infantry tank captured by German soldiers

Dunkirk, France

Gathering post for French prisoners of war

French prisoners of war

RIGHT: German soldiers with Algerian prisoners of war of the French colonial army

RIGHT: "Tales from the loo"

First Lieutenant Eizinger's grave

Burial site for fallen German WWI soldiers, Langemarck (Belgium)

Burial site of New Zealand soldiers who fell in WW I, Messine Ridge (Belgium)

Malo-les-Bains, Dunkirk

The French destroyer *L'Adroit* after a German attack. At noon on May 25, 1940, a German air raid destroyed this ship in Malo-les-Bains, near Dunkirk. It sank in shallow water.

LEFT: Willi Rose (right) and a friend RIGHT: Willi Rose

EASTERN FRONT

During the war in the Soviet Union, the Ninety-seventh Infantry Division had to cross several large rivers, including the Dniepr, Manytch, and Don.

The Dniepr River with a dam structure. The two taller rectangular structures on the left displayed colossal images of Lenin and Stalin.

Assault boats on what appears to be the Dniepr River

A Mercedes troop transporter

Destroyed German truck

TOP: German anti-tank crew with Ford trucks and anti-tank gun, model PAK 40. BOTTOM: German military truck with anti-tank gun (PAK 40).

German tanks (StG 40)

German tank (PzKpfw. IV)

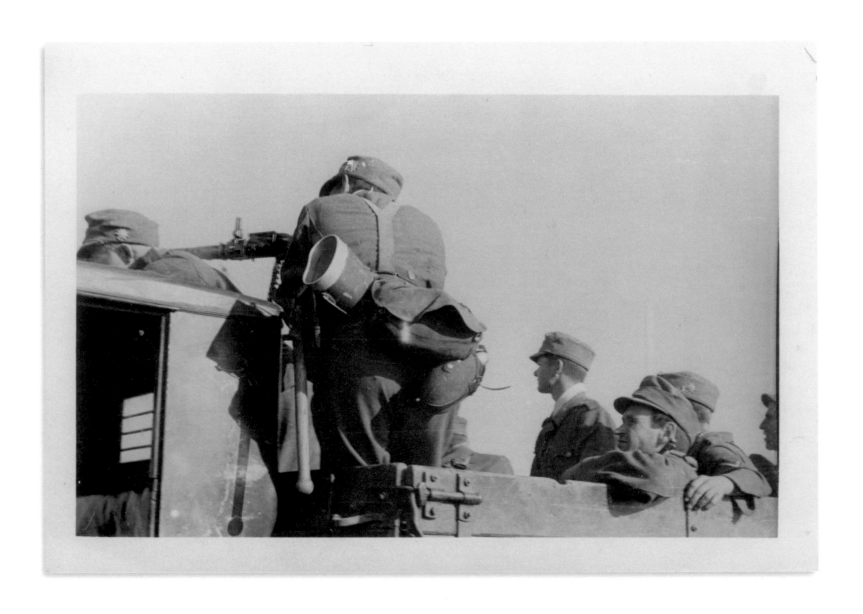

LEFT: Soldier with periscopic binoculars RIGHT: Lieutenant Colonel Friedrich-Wilhelm Otte, Pioneer Battalion of the Ninety-seventh Infantry Division

Soldier as a recon on a telegraph mast

TOP: German mountaineer with a K98 rifle BOTTOM: Anti-tank gun (PAK 40) with crew

German soldier with a K98 rifle

German military police talk to a civilian woman

Muddy tank road with trucks

Half-track motorcycle NSU 201 ZDB

Soldier laying telephone cable on the front

Field telephone

TOP AND MIDDLE: Bridge, probably over the Donez River

Road signs near Alexandrovka. Placed there by the "Transportation Regulatory Unit Kroitzsch," which was founded on the Manytch in July/August 1941.

Flood, likely after the retreating Soviet army bombed the Lake Manytch dam on July 27, 1941

Battle for Artemovsk, October 31, 1941

Roadsigns in Artemovsk. One of the road signs points to the town of Stupki (Ukraine), the site of a concentration camp

Magerov after the tank battle on June 25, 1941

After the battle of Magerov, June 25, 1941

Light infantry gun (le IG 18)

Russian arms looted on August 15, 1942, in Chirvanskaya, Caucasus

Overturned German tank (Panzerkampfwagen II Mod. C)

Anti-aircraft gun (Flakvierling 38)

Soviet reconnaissance aircraft

Soviet prisoners of war, probably near Podvysokoye

German soldiers guard Soviet prisoners of war and civilians

Soviet prisoners of war, probably near Podvysokoye

Soviet prisoner of war

Plank bearing the name of Captain Karl Langesee, Commander Second Infantry Regiment 207

Captain Karl Langesee decorated with the Knight's Cross of the Iron Cross, the highest medal for bravery

TOP: The Ninety-Seventh Infantry Division insignias ("Spielhahnfeder") BOTTOM: A road sign to the command office

All mines cleared

Soviet anti-tank and anti-personnel mines, types TM 38 and PMD 6

Road sign to the infirmary

Colonel Paul Heikaus's grave; "Mein Cheff" is handwritten on the back of the photograph

Dead Soviet soldier after German artillery fire

German aircraft

LEFT: Lieutenant Colonel Friedrich-Wilhelm Otte inspects mines RIGHT: General Ernst Rupp

General Ernst Rupp, commander of the Ninety-seventh Infantry Division

"I sat next to the general [Rupp], who was charming, shy and a little melancholic. I had the feeling his officers deeply loved him despite some eccentricities. Like *The Dead Souls*' Tchitchikov with his squires, I drive around here with the generals and observe their transformation into workers (...). They are specialists in the area of command technology and are, like the next best in the machine, expendable and replaceable."

—Ernst Jünger, *Strahlungen I, Kaukasische Aufzeichnungen* (Radiations I, Notes from the Caucases), December 19, 1942

TOP: Lieutenant General Maximilian de Angelis, XXXXIV. AK; and General Ernst Rupp, Ninety-seventh infantry division BOTTOM: General Ernst Rupp

LEFT: Lieutenant Colonel Friedrich-Wilhelm Otte with Captain Eberhard Mergner RIGHT: Lieutenant Colonel Friedrich-Wilhelm Otte with General Rupp

"We rested with Captain Mergener [*sic*], the leader of a squad. His command post revealed itself as a white house that lay like a forest ranger's station in a mud-covered clearing. In the middle of this wilderness, which was covered with the rubble of the war, we noticed a number of well-kept graves… the farmstead was encircled by deep shell holes, but the occupants had not yet moved out; the difference between the warm rooms and the inhospitable swamp is simply all too large."

—Ernst Jünger, *Strahlungen I, Kaukasische Aufzeichnungen* (Radiations I, Notes from the Caucasus), December 21, 1942

RIGHT: Willi Rose and a fellow soldier

Willi (with gun) at play

In the Kuban lowlands, Russia

The Monument to Artem (F. A. Sergeyev) in Artemowsk. Artem F. Sergeyev was one of the several thousand refugees who fled Russia after the end of the 1905 revolution and settled in Australia. When Sergeyev arrived in Brisbane in 1911, he decisively brought the Russian émigré community under Bolshevik influence; he established the Russian Workers Association and published several Bolshevik papers including *Izvestia*. He was a member of the Australian Socialist Party and was active in the local trade union movement. In May 1917, he returned to Russia and shortly thereafter became a member of the Central Committee of the Bolshevik Party. After the revolution, he was a member of the Central Executive Committee and a Commissar. He was also a member of the Executive Committee of the Communist International. He died in a train crash in 1921.

"The opponents expect no mercy from each other, and are supported in this opinion by propaganda. Last winter, a sled carrying wounded Russian officers accidentally ran into the German lines. The moment the passengers noticed this, they detonated their hand grenades between their bodies. Prisoners are after all taken to provide labor and also to attract deserters. Partisans, however, are outside the rules of war, in as much as one can still even speak of such laws. Like packs of wolves, they are surrounded to be exterminated. Here, I heard things that touch upon zoology."

—Ernst Jünger, *Strahlungen I, Kaukasische Aufzeichnungen* (Radiations I, Notes from the Caucasus, December 11, 1942

Willi on furlough in his hometown, Mürsbach, Franconia

Willi Rose and his motorcycle

Last visit home in late 1944 or early 1945, before the last months of war and captivity in the Carpathian mountains

BIBLIOGRAPHY

Dewitz, Bodo von, ed. *Kiosk. Eine Geschichte der Fotoreportage 1839–1973* (A History of Photo Reportage). Göttingen: Steidl Verlag, 2001.

Frerk, Willy. "Das Erlebnis des Einzelnen ist zu einem Volkserlebnis geworden, und das durch die Kamera!" (The experience of the individual has now become an experience of the people, through the camera!). In *Photofreund* (1933): 417–418.

Hamburger Institut für Sozialforschung (Hamburg Institute for Social Research). *Vernichtungskrieg. Verbrechen der Wehrmacht 1941 bis 1944* (The German Army and Genocide. Crimes Against War Prisoners, Jews, and other Civilians in the East, 1939–1944. New York: The New Press, 1999). Exh. cat. Hamburg: Hamburger Editions, 1996.

Hamburger Institut für Sozialforschung (Hamburg Institute for Social Research). *Eine Ausstellung und ihre Folgen. Zur Rezeption der Ausstellung "Vernichtungskrieg. Verbrechen der Wehrmacht 1941 bis 1944"* (An Exhibition and Its Outcome. On the Reception of the Exhibition "War of Annihilation. Crimes Committed by the Wehrmacht 1941–1944"). Hamburg: Hamburger Editions, 1999.

Hamburger Institut für Sozialforschung (Hamburg Institute for Social Research). *Verbrechen der Wehrmacht. Dimensionen des Vernichtungskriegs 1941–1944* (Crimes of the German Wehrmacht. Dimensions of a War of Annihilation 1941–1944). Exh. cat. Hamburg: Hamburger Editions, 2002.

Henisch, Peter. *Die kleine Figur meines Vaters* (The Little Figure of My Father). Salzburg: Residenz Verlag, 2003.

Holzer, Anton, ed. *Mit der Kamera bewaffnet. Krieg und Fotografie* (Armed with the Camera. War and Photography). Marburg: Jonas Verlag, 2003.

Hummel, Alexander. "Fotografieren im Kriegssommer 1940" (Taking Photos in the Summer of War 1940). *Photoblätter* 7, vol. 17, (1940): 121–122.

Hüppauf, Bernd. "Der entleerte Blick hinter der Kamera" (The Empty Glance behind the Camera). In *Vernichtungskrieg. Verbrechen der Wehrmacht 1941 bis 1944* (War of Annihilation. Crimes Committed by the Wehrmacht 1941–1944), eds. H. Heer and K. Naumann. Hamburg: Hamburger Institut für Sozialforschung, 1995, pp. 504–527.

Jahn, Peter, and Ulrike Schmiegelt, eds. *Foto-Feldpost. Geknipste Kriegserlebnisse 1939–1945* (Photo Army Mail. Snapshots of War Experiences). Berlin: Elefanten Presse, 2000.

Jünger, Ernst. *Strahlungen I. Kaukasische Aufzeichnungen* (Radiations I. Notes from the Caucasus). Munich: Deutscher Taschenbuch Verlag, 1988.

Koristka, Josef. "Unsere Frauen – sollten mehr photographieren" (Our women–should take more photos). *Photoblätter* (1939): 334–336.

"Kunst und Krieg" (Art and War). *Kunstforum*, vol. 165 (2003).
Milton, Sybil. "The Camera as Weapon: Documentary Photography and the Holocaust." *Simon Wiesenthal Center Annual* 1 (1984): 45–68.

Ott, Ernst-Ludwig. *Die Spielhahnjäger 1940–1945. Bilddokumentation der 97. Jäger-Division* (The Black Cock Hunters 1940–1945. Picture Documentation of the 97th Hunter Division). Friedberg: Podzun-Pallas Verlag, 1982.

Ott, Ernst. *Jäger am Feind. Geschichte und Opfergang der 97. Jäger-Division 1940–1945.* (Hunter of the Enemy. History and Sacrifices of the 97th Hunter Division 1940–1945). Munich, 1966.

Paul, Jean. *Vorschule der Ästhetik* (Preschool of Aesthetics). 1. Abteilung, III. Prog., § 14, Hamburg: Meiner Verlag, 1990.

Reetz, Wilhelm, ed. *Eine ganze Welt gegen uns. Eine Geschichte des Weltkriegs in Bildern* (A Whole World against Us. A History of the World War in Images). Berlin: Ullstein Verlag, 1934.

Sachsse, Rolf. *Die Erziehung zum Wegsehen. Fotografie im NS-Staat* (Educated to Look Away. Photography in the NS State). Dresden: Philo Fine Arts, 2003.

Sebald, W. G. *Die Ausgewanderten* (The Emigrants). Frankfurt/M.: Fischer Verlag, 2003.

Stadelmann, Christian, and Regina Wonisch, eds. *Brutale Neugier. Walter Henisch, Kriegsfotograf und Bildreporter* (Brutal Curiosity. Walter Henisch, War Photographer and Photo Reporter). Vienna: Brandstätter Verlag, 2003.

Starke, Herbert. "Und trotzdem: Amateurfotografie!" (And Despite It All: Amateur Photography!). *Photofreund* (1939): 349–50.

Starl, Timm. *Knipser. Die Bildgeschichte der privaten Fotografie in Deutschland und Österreich von 1880 bis 1980* (Snapshooters. The History of Private Photography in Germany and Austria 1880–1980 in Images). Munich: Koehler and Amelang, 1995.

Stephainsky, Hans. "Innere Erneuerung der Photographie" (The Inner Reformation of Photography). *Satrap* (1933): 225–230.

Stiewe, Willy. *Foto und Volk* (Photo and the People). Halle N. P., 1933.